owning a pet

HAMSTER

Selina Wood

FRANKLIN WATTS

LONDON•SYDNEY

First published in 2005 by
Franklin Watts
96 Leonard Street
London
EC2A 4XD

Franklin Watts Australia
45–51 Huntley Street
Alexandria, NSW 2015

© Franklin Watts 2005

Series editor: Adrian Cole
Series design: Sarah Borny
Art director: Jonathan Hair
Picture researcher: Kathy Lockley
Illustrations by: Hannah Matthews

A CIP catalogue record for this book is
available from the British Library.

ISBN: 0 7496 5927 0

Dewey Classification: 636.9'356

Printed in China

The author and publisher would like to thank the following people
and hamsters for their contribution to the production of this book:

Anna Broke; James Campbell and Harry; Rachel Lefeaver and Avril

Acknowledgements:

Arco/F. Lukasseck/Alamy 8 & Cover.
Mary Evans Picture Library 6 bl. Che German/Alamy 23 t.
Getty Images 6 rc. Angela Hampton/RSPCA Photolibrary 28 bl.
Lorraine Hill/Acorn Stock images 6 tl, 7, 10, 11, 12 t, 12 b, 13, 16 rc,
17, 21 bl, 25 t, 26 t, 27 t, 28 rc. Adelle Homer 14 b, 22, 23 b,
24 b, 25 b, 29. Scott Hortop/Alamy 5. Ernie Janes/NHPA 14 t.
Yves Lanceau/NHPA 9 t. Ray Moller 1, 16 tl, 16 b, 18 rc,
18 tl, 19 t, 20, 21 t. Carlos Sanz/VWPics/Alamy 9 b.
Jorg & Petra Wegner/Bruce Coleman 27 b.
Max Weinzierl/Alamy 4, 15,19 rc, 24 t, 26 b.

Whilst every attempt has been made to clear copyright
should there be any inadvertent omission please apply
in the first instance to the publisher regarding rectification.

Contents

Pet hamsters

Hamsters are active and inquisitive. They make good pets because they are fascinating animals, but they need the care and attention of a good owner.

Owning a hamster

Owning a hamster is a big responsibility, even if a hamster is quite small. Amongst other things it will depend on you to feed it, clean out its cage, and protect it. A hamster also needs mental stimulation otherwise it becomes bored. A hamster is not just there to entertain you – it has a life too. You have a duty to provide the best possible care.

Before you buy

Think about whether you and your family can take on the commitment of a hamster. Hamsters have characteristics of their own that may not fit in with the way you live. They are nocturnal (active at night), so they need peace and quiet during the day. If frightened, they may become aggressive, and they have short lifespans – only about two years.

RODENTS

Hamsters are rodents – mammals with sharp, constantly growing front teeth used for gnawing. Mice, rats, squirrels and beavers are also rodents. Rodents tend to breed often and have large numbers of young, and many build nests and burrows.

All hamsters sleep during the day and are active at night.

Where can I get a hamster?

Look for a hamster breeder in your area. This is the place to buy a hamster because it will be healthy and well cared for. A good breeder will also be able to answer your questions about hamster care. You could get a hamster from an animal rescue centre, although you are less likely to be able to find out about the hamster's history. Ask staff at the centre about the hamster and find out as much as you can about it. Try to choose one that is young and that doesn't seem to be aggressive.

Hamsters are great fun and make good companions.

QUESTIONS TO ASK A BREEDER

● How old is the hamster?

● Does it like to be handled?

● What does it like to eat?

● Can I see the parents?

● Can I see where the hamster has been kept?

WHAT TO LOOK FOR

Buy a hamster that's aged between 5 and 12 weeks – they are easier to tame than older ones. Adult hamsters make good pets if they've already had plenty of contact with humans. A healthy hamster should have glossy fur, no patches or rashes on the skin and clean eyes, nose, ears, mouth and rear.

Hamster history

Until the 1930s, hamsters could only be seen in zoos, laboratories or in the wild. They were not thought of as pets, largely because they were difficult to breed in captivity.

Hamster testing

During the 1920s, scientists in Israel used Chinese hamsters for tests in laboratories (right). However, these hamsters failed to breed successfully, so the scientists looked for another type of hamster for their experiments.

An illustration showing Golden (Syrian) hamsters in the wild.

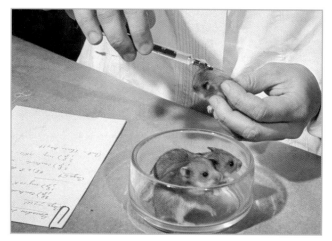

Golden discovery

In 1930, scientists discovered a mother and litter of Golden hamsters (Syrian hamsters) near Mount Aleppo in Syria. They were taken into captivity where they bred very easily. It wasn't until seven years later that descendants of the original wild litter were transported to England and North America where they were bred as pets. These are the ancestors of most of the pet Syrian hamsters in the world today.

"Hamster shows are great places to pick up advice from more experienced owners."

Show hamsters are measured and checked following strict rules.

Pet potential

Following the success of the domestication of Syrian hamsters, Chinese hamsters were introduced to the pet trade in the 1960s, and the Dwarf Russian in the 1970s. Roborovski hamsters became pets in the 1990s. Today, the hamster is the most popular rodent to be kept as a pet.

Hamsters on show

Some hamsters are bred purely for exhibiting at shows. These hamsters are the best examples of their breed. Judges look at the size, markings and general condition of a hamster before deciding on a winner. If you are keen to find out more about breeds of hamsters, you could go to a hamster show to see the different varieties. That way you will find out more about the breeds, and you may pick up a few tips from the experts.

In the wild

Only a few types of hamster are kept as pets. Most live in the wild in elaborate burrows or nests in semi-desert areas or mountainous regions of China, North Africa, the Middle East, Eastern Europe and Russia.

Wild Syrian hamsters live in North Africa and the Middle East. They sleep underground in burrows during the day to keep out of the hot sun. At night, when the desert cools down, they come out to search for food. Morning dew is their main source of water.

Wild Dwarf Campbells Russian hamsters are found in the steppes region of Russia. They dig burrows in the ground and line their nests with grass to keep warm. Temperatures outside can drop to around -15°C in the winter, while inside the burrow stays at around 16°C.

Wild Roborovskis, like wild Chinese hamsters, live in the deserts of Northern China. Roborovski burrows are often among the deepest, some as far down as 4 metres.

This wild Syrian hamster is standing on its back legs to get a better view of its surroundings.

"The word hamster comes from the German word 'hamstern', which means 'to hoard'."

Finding food

Hamsters in the wild feed at night on a wide range of seeds, roots and sometimes insects. They travel up to 2 kilometres at night in search of things to eat. Hamsters carry food in their cheek pouches until they reach the safety of their nest, where they eat or store it. Most hamsters live in harsh conditions where there isn't much food, so they hoard it when they find a lot.

Hamsters love all kinds of seeds. Their sharp teeth are perfect for splitting open the shells.

Predators

All wild hamsters are under constant danger from predators, such as birds of prey, foxes, stoats and weasels. They can be attacked when out looking for food or when inside their burrows. Hamsters build burrow networks with many exits and entrances so that they can make a quick escape.

This weasel is one of the hamster's main predators.

Which breed?

Before you choose a hamster, it is important to know as much as possible about how the different breeds look and behave. This will help you to find the perfect hamster for your lifestyle.

SYRIAN

Syrian hamsters are the most common hamster pets. Their natural colour is rich golden brown with a white underside, although there are now over 100 colour varieties. A few varieties have long coats and need regular grooming. Syrians prefer to live on their own. They fight if they are put in the same cage as another hamster.

Size: .... **15–20 cm**
Sociable: .... **No**
Difficulty level: .... **Easy**
Lifespan: .... **2–2.5 years**
Agouti colours (see opposite page) include: .... **Cinnamon, golden, grey, rust, yellow**
Good choice as a first pet hamster? .... **Yes!**

This is a cinnamon-coloured Syrian hamster. Many Syrian hamsters are a single colour, others are albino (white) and some have a marked coat.

Chinese hamsters are about the same size as mice and were the first hamsters to be kept in captivity.

CHINESE

The first Chinese hamsters were captured in Beijing and it wasn't long before they were exported to other countries for tests in laboratories. Chinese hamsters are smaller than Syrians and have greyish brown coats with a dark stripe down their backs. Some can live with other hamsters if they have grown up together, but most of them will fight and need to be kept individually. In the wild, Chinese hamsters breed very quickly, although they are very difficult to breed in captivity. They are more timid than other types but may be less likely to nip.

Size:	**10–12 cm**
Sociable:	**No**
Difficulty level:	**Medium**
Lifespan:	**2–2.5 years**
Colours:	**Normal and agouti**
Good choice as a first pet hamster?	**Yes!**

AGOUTI MARKINGS

'Agouti' is the natural pattern of fur that occurs in wild hamsters. An agouti hamster has a coat that is a darker colour at the roots and lighter at the ends. It is an off-white colour underneath and has a dark line down the centre of its back.

Which breed?

Dwarf Campbells Russian hamsters have short, dense, brown fur, with a dark stripe running between their eyes and down their backs.

Size: .... **10–12 cm**

Sociable: .... **Yes**

Difficulty level: .... **Medium**

Lifespan: .... **1.5–2 years**

Good choice as
a first pet hamster? .... **Yes!**

DWARF CAMPBELLS RUSSIAN

These hamsters, often sold as 'Djungarian' hamsters, are the most popular of the two Dwarf Russian species. They have hairy feet and large cheek pouches. Most Dwarf Campbells Russians can live in single-sex pairs or mixed groups without fighting. They are not afraid of people, although they must be handled confidently. They can easily escape from some hamster cages, so keep them in a cage with smaller bar spacing, such as one designed for mice.

DWARF WINTER WHITE RUSSIAN

This Russian species is also sometimes sold as 'Siberian' or 'Djungarian'. They are about the same size as Dwarf Campbells Russians, which makes them difficult to tell apart, but are slightly less round. They can easily escape from cages with normal bar spacing, but are less likely to nip an inexperienced owner. In the wild, Dwarf Winter White Russians turn white during the winter.

Size: .... **8–10 cm**

Sociable: .... **Yes**

Difficulty level: .... **Medium**

Lifespan: .... **1.5–2 years**

Good choice as
a first pet hamster? .... **Yes!**

ROBOROVSKI

This is the smallest and fastest type of hamster that can be kept as a pet, and is very difficult to handle. For this reason experts do not recommend a Roborovski as a first hamster, although more experienced owners will enjoy their good natures and tidy habits. They have distinctive white eyebrows and sandy-coloured fur. Roborovskis can live with other hamsters if socialised at a young age, but are very rarely sold unless through a specialist breeder.

Size:	**4–5 cm**
Sociable:	**Yes**
Difficulty level:	**Hard**
Lifespan:	**3–3.5 years**
Good choice as a first pet hamster?	**No!**

MALE OR FEMALE?

You may need to get help from the rescue centre staff or breeder to identify the sex of your hamster. There is little difference between the behaviour of male and female hamsters, but females have a more rounded body than males. If you don't want your hamsters to breed, do not put a male and female together.

Creating a home

When you first take your hamster home it will feel anxious and nervous. Give it time to settle into its new home. Have everything ready before it arrives so it is disturbed as little as possible.

Cage or 'aquarium'

Buy as large a cage as possible – at least 75 x 40 x 40 cm – and make sure it has the correct bar spacing for your type of hamster. Don't buy a round cage, as many people believe it can cause hamsters distress. The cage should have a tough, metal top with several doors to allow easy access. Make sure they can be shut securely though!

The base should be made of strong plastic. You can also buy glass or plastic 'aquariums' that are better suited for Dwarf hamsters. Never keep a hamster in a wooden cage or hutch.

Tunnels and ladders

Tunnels provide your hamster with an environment similar to the one it would experience in the wild. Hamsters love to store food and bedding in tunnels, and they make them feel more secure. Ladders allow your hamster to access different levels of its cage. By moving up and down the hamster also gets exercise.

Ladders should be positioned in the cage to avoid the risk of your hamster falling and injuring itself.

Tunnel networks like this are great fun for your hamster, but harder for you to clean.

BEDDING

Put about 2–3 cm of non-toxic wood shavings at the bottom of the cage (below). You could also add a layer of hay or straw. Always use hamster bedding, never cotton wool, fine sawdust, newspaper or cat litter – they can harm your hamster.

CAGE POSITION

Don't put the cage anywhere it can be easily knocked over. Put it somewhere draught-free, warm, and out of direct sunlight. Have it somewhere visible, but maybe not in your bedroom as hamsters make a lot of noise at night. It should also be placed where other pets, such as dogs, can't get access to the hamster.

SECURITY ALERT!
Make sure your hamster is kept in a secure cage with no holes that it can squeeze through. Hamsters are very good at escaping. Check the condition of the cage regularly to make sure it is still escape proof and that the doors are firmly secured.

ACCESSORIES

Five essential accessories to make your hamster feel at home:

- A nesting box will provide your hamster with the added comfort of somewhere to make its nest. It won't always use it; some hamsters prefer to make their nest in tunnels if they have them. But it can also be useful to keep your hamster in when you clean out its cage (see page 20).

- A food bowl. It should be heavy and shallow to stop your hamster knocking the food over.

- A drip-feed water bottle is the best way to give your hamster a supply of water (see page 17).

- You might find your hamster enjoys running on a wheel. This is not just for your entertainment; it's a good way for it to exercise, too.

- A gnawing block can provide a welcome distraction from the plastic tunnels and other accessories in the cage. It also helps your hamster to keep its teeth in top shape.

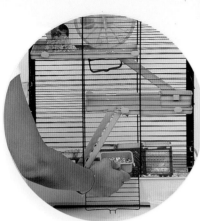

Feeding time

You must feed your hamster once, at the same time, every day. The best time to feed it is in the early evening, when it begins to wake up.

Healthy diet

Good quality hamster food mix has the right mixture of grains, seeds and nuts and can be bought at most pet shops. However, you also need to feed your hamster fruit and vegetables, but do not feed it too much or it may get an upset stomach. Try two or three pieces a week to start with (see panel opposite). This balanced diet is essential for a healthy hamster.

Small amounts of fresh fruit and vegetables.

Loose, pre-mixed dry food.

Dry food bar – something for your hamster to chew on.

"Never give your hamster sweets. They could easily get stuck in its mouth or throat."

Water

Make sure your hamster has a constant supply of fresh water to drink. Don't assume because it is a desert animal that it can go without. A drip-feed water bottle keeps the water cleaner than if you use a dish. Keep the bottle topped up, and wash it out thoroughly once or twice a week with a non-toxic detergent.

Drinking from a drip-feed water bottle. Make sure it's positioned where your hamster can always reach it.

Never feed your hamster chocolate, kidney beans, onions, rhubarb or tomato seeds. Follow the list below or ask a vet for advice if you are still unsure.

LIST OF TREATS

Hamsters love these foods in small amounts:

Acorns	**Cheese**	**Hard-boiled egg**
Apples	**Cold toast**	**Peas**
Bananas	**Courgettes**	**Potato**
Broccoli	**Cucumber**	**Spinach**
Carrots	**Dandelions**	**Sweetcorn**
Cauliflower	**Dog biscuits**	**Turnips**
Celery	**Grapes**	**Watercress**

New skills

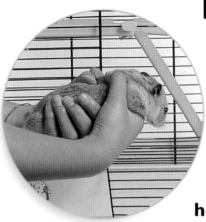

Bonding with your hamster will not happen overnight. It is a gradual process that will depend very much on your understanding of how to handle and respond to it properly.

HOLDING YOUR HAMSTER

Hamsters do not enjoy being handled too often. Don't handle it when it's asleep: you could surprise it and be on the receiving end of a sharp nip! Slowly tame your hamster by stroking and talking to it when you feed it. Try encouraging it to walk onto your hands. If it still tries to nip, stroke it wearing a pair of new, strong gloves (right). It will learn that you are not going to attack.

HANDLING DO'S AND DON'TS

- Do talk to your hamster and make slow movements when feeding it

- Do wash your hands before handling your hamster to remove food smells. You should wash them afterwards, too

- Do establish a feeding and playing routine with your hamster

- Don't pick up a sleeping hamster

- Don't surprise a hamster by making loud noises or knocking its home

- Don't hold a hamster too tightly, you could injure it

- Never hold a hamster more than 20 cm above the ground. It could jump if it becomes frightened and fall

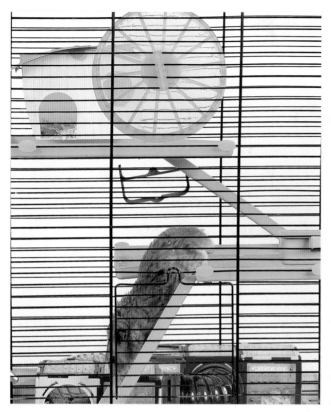

Night-time athletes

Hamsters sleep during the day and are very active at night: climbing, burrowing, scratching and running. Try not to disturb your hamster too much during the day, which is its natural resting time. Instead, build your routine around its behaviour. Set a regular time in the evening when you feed and play with your hamster. Clean out its cage early in the morning or late in the evening.

HAMSTER HABITS

These are some of the habits you'll see when you watch your hamster.

Nesting

Nesting is one of a hamster's strongest instincts. Your hamster will gather up nesting material to make cosy hiding places, so make sure it has some hay.

Scent communication

Hamsters, like many desert animals, communicate and mark their territory with scent from glands around their eyes, ears and rear. You'll notice them rubbing themselves against things – including you!

Self grooming

You will often see your hamster grooming (right). It uses its front paws to rub and wash its face and its sharp teeth to untangle fur. Long-haired hamsters need extra grooming (see page 21).

Squealing

Your hamster might squeal when you try to pick it up or if it thinks it is threatened. Wait for it to calm down before trying to handle it.

Hamster care

To keep your hamster healthy you need to keep its home clean and dry. Occasionally, you may need to clean its coat as well. Long-haired hamsters need regular grooming.

Daily clean-out

It is essential to clean out uneaten food from your hamster's home every day. This will help to prevent a build-up of germs and reduce the chance of your hamster becoming ill. Remove most urine-soaked wood shavings, but leave some in one corner, well away from your hamster's food. It will start to use this area as a toilet. When you add new bedding, keep some of the old shavings in there. The familiar smell will make your hamster feel less distressed.

Use special hamster bedding – some wood contains toxic chemicals.

Wash the cage

Your hamster's home should be completely cleaned out every week. Throw out the old bedding and wash the cage with non-toxic detergent. Then put in clean shavings and bedding. While you are cleaning the cage, you can put the hamster in a safe place (such as a well-ventilated box) or in an exercise ball, which you can buy from a pet shop. Make sure your hamster is supervised while in the ball and don't leave it in there for too long. Your hamster will become overheated and could die.

"Harry loves to be groomed. He just sits in my hand sniffing and looking around him."

Grooming

To groom your hamster, use a soft, dry toothbrush, always taking care to avoid its eyes. Short-haired hamsters only need grooming when they get unusually dirty. Never give your hamster a bath or get it excessively wet. It could go into shock or catch pneumonia. For dirt that is difficult to remove, use a damp toothbrush.

Sit on the floor while brushing and holding your hamster carefully.

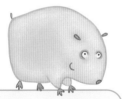

LONG-HAIRED HAMSTERS

Long-haired hamsters need grooming often, as their coats easily become matted and tangled up with bedding. Aim to groom your hamster every other day, so you can keep its dense coat in perfect condition. Be gentle when you do this as the hairs are fine and straggly.

Staying safe

Hamsters are extremely cute, loveable animals, but they are also small and vulnerable. They can be easily injured or become ill if they are not kept safe.

FALLS

Hamsters are short-sighted, so even if they are kept properly, they may suffer from falls. Falls can be serious because hamsters have very fragile bones. If a hamster falls, return it to its nest and monitor its behaviour. You should stop it trying to climb by removing ladders, wheels or other toys from its home. If you have a cage, place the hamster in an aquarium-style home or temporarily in a ventilated box. Transfer bedding from its home to make it feel secure. If it hasn't recovered in an hour, take it to a vet.

INJURY

Occasionally, hamsters are injured during an attack from other hamsters or as a result of escaping. A hamster will be very shocked at first. It should be put back in its nest to recover, but in a separate home away from other hamsters. If the hamster has a small cut or bite it will lick and clean it. If it has more serious injuries, such as a wound that is bleeding heavily, it must be taken to a vet straightaway.

HIBERNATION AND OVERHEATING

If a hamster is not kept in a room with a balanced temperature (around 20°C) it may begin to hibernate if it is too cold, or overheat if it is too warm.

Hibernation – the hamster doesn't move but is still breathing. Move the hamster in its home to a warmer room. Provide it with plenty of bedding and maintain a warm room temperature.

Overheating – the hamster shivers and moves slowly. Move the hamster in its home to a cooler room and splash it with a little water. Make sure its water bottle is topped up with fresh water.

These hamsters are sleeping. Always keep the room temperature balanced to stop them hibernating or overheating.

POISONOUS SPRAYS

Before using an aerosol spray, check the manufacturer's instructions to make sure it is safe to use around animals. Hamsters are sensitive to poisoning. They lick unhealthy substances that have stuck to their fur when they groom.

If you are worried about your hamster, take it to your vet for a check-up.

Staying healthy

Pet hamsters come into contact with more germs than their wild relations because they are near humans. There are no vaccinations for hamsters, so you must be alert to any signs of ill-health.

Check-up

Examine your hamster regularly (below). Check that its ears are clean and do not smell. Its eyes should be bright and shiny. Look inside its mouth and check its cheek pouches. The lining is delicate and can get damaged very easily. If any material gets stuck in the pouches for a long period, get advice from your vet.

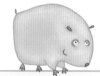

SIGNS OF ILLNESS

If you suspect your hamster may be ill, take it to the vet immediately. Small animals, such as hamsters, can become ill very quickly.

Signs of illness include:

- **strange or unusual breathing**
- **cloudy eyes**
- **raised fur or loss of fur**
- **sore spots on its skin**
- **diarrhoea (very runny faeces)**
- **runny nose**
- **loss of appetite**
- **unusual lack of energy**

Teeth and claw check

Your hamster should have a gnawing block to keep its teeth short and sharp. Check that its teeth and claws are growing properly and are not broken or overgrown. Ask your vet to show you how to cut them. Cutting them incorrectly can hurt your hamster.

Let your hamster out for a run in a hamster-proof room. You must always watch your hamster carefully when you allow it out.

Hamsters chew and gnaw most things. This natural wear should keep their teeth healthy, but they still need to be checked.

Exercise

Your hamster will get exercise by using its wheel or exercise ball, but many owners feel confident enough to let their hamsters out in a secure room. There is always a risk if you do this, but by making the room hamster-proof, this risk should be kept to a minimum. Block up any holes in the room, such as behind cabinets, sofas, etc. Cover electric wires in strong plastic tubing to reduce the risk of the hamster chewing through them. Move plants to where your hamster cannot reach them and give it plenty of chew toys and cardboard tubes to play with. Always keep other animals out of the room while your hamster is running around.

Breeding?

**Hamsters have a short lifespan
of about two to three years.
You might be tempted to let
your hamster breed during this
time, but it is a huge responsibility.**

Think carefully

Before you put a male and female
hamster together, think very carefully
about what will happen.

First you will need two suitable
hamsters that will be able to breed
together safely. Some pairings must be
avoided because the puppies will die at
birth. You also need extra feed for the
puppies, somewhere to house them
and to find good homes for them all.

*Think very carefully before you
allow a male and female hamster
together. Don't forget:
irresponsible breeding is cruel.*

These pups are about two weeks old. Their eyes have opened and their hair has grown. Both of them have a new home to go to.

Pairing

Syrian hamsters usually fight when they get together to breed and may have up to 20 pups in one litter. Russian and Chinese hamsters mate more peacefully, but they reproduce extremely quickly. They may have around 8 pups at one time. By the time they are 2 months old, Syrian pups need cages of their own otherwise they fight.

A female dwarf hamster in the wild will mate again as soon as 24 hours after giving birth!

Dealing with loss

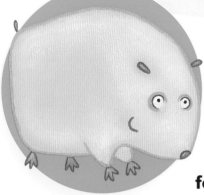

You will develop a close friendship with your hamster over time, but eventually it will die, as all pets do. Take good care of your hamster through its lifetime, so your feelings of loss will be less distressing.

Getting older

As your hamster gets older, like the one on the right, it may begin to slow down, lose its fur, become blind, suffer from dry skin and lose weight. Be sensitive to it and don't force it to exercise or play. When your hamster finally dies you will feel sad, but at least you will have made the most of your time together.

ESCAPE PLANS

If you lose your hamster because it escapes, try putting the open cage on the floor with food inside. Alternatively, put some food in a bucket in a dark corner and add a ramp. Your hamster will smell the food, climb the ramp and fall into the bucket. Line the bucket with a towel so your hamster doesn't hurt itself when it falls.

"Avril is so cool, I love her to bits. She always does something silly to make me laugh!" Rachel

Accidents and illness

If you are unlucky and your hamster dies in an accident or from illness, try not to blame yourself. The chances are there was nothing you or anyone else could have done to prevent it. You may feel that its death was unfair. This is quite a natural feeling of grief. Talk to people about how you are feeling – it usually helps.

TIME TO REMEMBER

Write a story about your hamster:

"I will never forget the day I brought Nibbles home. I thought he was the best in the litter because he was cuter than the others, with big eyes and funny tufts of hair on his back. The first day he stayed huddled up in his bedding and wouldn't come out at all. Then during the night I heard a scratching noise. It was really funny. I realised he was beginning to explore. After a few days, I knew Nibbles was a bit crazy because he made his bed at the bottom of his wheel, not in his nest box...."

Enjoying good times with a friend. You'll have many happy memories to look back on.

Happy memories

A memorial service in your garden is a good way of showing respect to your dead hamster. You may want to write a special poem in its memory, or a story recounting your friendship, with photos and pictures. Remember to include all the good times.

Glossary

Agouti: Fur with alternate dark and light bands on each hair – as it would appear in the wild.

Aquarium-style home: A home in the style of an aquarium, made of glass or plastic, as opposed to a cage with bars. Aquarium homes are suitable for Dwarf hamsters, which can slip through cage bars.

Breed: A group of animals within the same species whose characteristics are passed down from generation to generation. Also means to mate and have offspring, and to organise the reproduction of breeds.

Breeder: A person or organisation that breeds a particular type of animal.

Distress: Pain, disturbance, discomfort caused by bad care.

Domestication: The taming of animals to keep them as pets or farm animals.

Gnawing block: A block made of hardwood for a hamster to wear down its teeth on.

Hoard: A hamster's stock of food; also means to accumulate and store.

Mammal: Animals that are warm-blooded, have hair and produce milk to feed their young.

Non-toxic: Not poisonous.

Pneumonia: A dangerous lung infection.

Rodents: Small mammals – the most numerous and widespread of all mammals – that have large gnawing teeth.

Semi-desert: Dry regions that share some characteristics with deserts, but have more rainfall and plants.

Species: A group of animals that have characteristics in common, distinct from other animals, and that can reproduce together.

Vaccination: A medical treatment to prevent an animal from getting a disease, often in the form of an injection. Also called a jab.

Variety: A particular type of hamster, usually a colour type within a breed.

Websites

If you want to learn more about hamster breeds, buying hamsters, keeping hamsters or to become involved in animal welfare, there are several helpful organisations you can contact. Your local pet centre can provide information about groups in your area. Try the Internet, too – some useful websites are listed here.

www.hamsters-uk.org
Website of the National Hamster Council – the oldest hamster club in the world. Features information on hamster breeds, clubs and a section with frequently asked questions.

www.petwebsite.com/hamsters
The hamster section of this large website, with information to help you buy, care for and show all kinds of hamster. It also has a picture gallery.

www.hamsterific.com
Website dedicated to hamsters, featuring diet information, a home and bedding guide, health care tips, a picture gallery and frequently asked questions.

www.hamsters.co.uk
This website features lots of tips for keeping your hamster healthy, including illustrated guides. It also features handling information.

www.hamsterland.com
Hamster heaven! Lots of information about hamster history, care, handling, feeding, grooming, health, diseases and more.

More general information on the care, health and welfare of pets is available from a number of organisations. These include:

www.rspca.org.uk
www.rspca.org.au
News articles, rehoming information and animal care advice from the Royal Society for the Prevention of Cruelty to Animals.

www.peta.org
Website of People for the Ethical Treatment of Animals – the largest animals rights group in the world. Contains information promoting the safety and responsible treatment of all animals.

www.aspca.org
The American Society for the Prevention of Cruelty to Animals website features a wide range of information, from advice about pet care to campaigns fighting animal cruelty.

Every effort has been made by the Publishers to ensure that these websites contain no inappropriate or offensive material. However, because of the nature of the Internet, it is impossible to guarantee that the contents of these sites will not be altered. We strongly advise that Internet access is supervised by a responsible adult.

Index